28 TIPS TO BECOME A Great GRANDPA

28 TIPS TO BECOME A Great GRANDPA

LORIN BARBER

Bonneville Books
Springville, Utah

ISBN 13: 978-1-59955-357-3

Published by Bonneville Books, an imprint of Cedar Fort, Inc., 2373 W. 700 S., Springville, UT 84663
Distributed by Cedar Fort, Inc. www.cedarfort.com

LIBRARY OF CONGRESS CATALOGING-IN-PUBLICATION DATA

Barber, Lorin K. (Lorin Keith), 1952- author.
28 tips to become a great grandpa / Lorin K. Barber.
pages cm
ISBN 978-1-59955-357-3
1. Grandparent and child. I. Title.
BF723.G68B37 2010
649'.1--dc22
2010042744

Cover design by Angela D. Olsen
Cover Illustration by Melissa Bastow
Cover design © 2011 by Lyle Mortimer
Edited and typeset by Heidi Doxey

Printed in the United States of America

10 9 8 7 6 5 4 3 2 1

Printed on acid-free paper

To Avery, Grace, Coby, Calvin,
Elliot, Chase, River, and Penelope

Author's Note

This book contains very little of what it takes to be a great grandfather. On the other hand, it has everything that's necessary. Its purpose is to spur you to customize your grandfathering. It's a bit of wit, a bit of wisdom, and hopefully a lot of thought provocation.

I've tried to pen a short insight into some different aspects of grandkids' lives that a grandpa should influence. I've created space for a grandpa to ponder the things in his life and his times that should become his grandchildren's history—not world history, not national history, but family history.

Grandchildren need to know what makes them who they are. This may include being American, British, or

Japanese, but it absolutely includes being your grandchild. I hope you will give them a sense of you, a sense of history, and a sense of themselves. Give them "roots." Give them the foundation they need to be their best selves. That foundation can't be complete without a strong grandfather figure. Let that figure be you.

Last, don't think anything in this book implies that I believe myself to be a great grandpa. It merely means I have contemplated and continue to contemplate the kind of grandpa I'd like to be.

Table of Contents

Introduction

I've written this book attempting to encourage grandpas, including myself, to be the best they can be. The world today is fast paced, computerized, and highly stressful. Kids need a break. Kids need peace. Kids need a grandpa.

Slow down your grandkids. It will require a Herculean effort, especially once they hit teenage years. The younger you start, the better chance you'll have. The best opportunity is when you have them cornered: at bedtime, in the car, or outdoors alone with you. Aside from those quiet moments, your words won't be heard, and your actions will have to speak for you.

Be fun, be interesting, and be there. For every hour you grab their attention, you may get in one word of pure teaching. They need you. They need your wisdom. They need the roots you can pass on to anchor them against the floods of modern mayhem.

In writing this book, I've reviewed my own need for improvement. No one should expect perfection, but somehow grandkids will often see it in you. I did with my grandpas.

Rules

• • • • • •

1. Always obey Grandma—except when she's not looking.

J.C. Watts said, "Character is doing the right thing when nobody's looking." These are wise words, but for grandpas, I prefer the statement, "Fun happens when nobody's looking."

2. Always obey the rules parents have set down for their children—except when the parents aren't looking.

I love this quote by Sam Levenson: "The reason grandchildren and grandparents get along so well is that they have a common enemy."

3. Always act with the decorum befitting your age—except when no other adults are looking.

Ogden Nash once said, "When grandparents enter the door, discipline flies out the window." In the same vein, Gene Perret said, "Grandparents are there to help children get into mischief they haven't thought of yet."

4. Don't be a grouchy, grumpy grandpa!

If you can't stand noise, get over it. If a messy house makes you crabby, get over it. If your grandchild's words or actions bother you, get over it. There is no excuse for a grouchy, grumpy grandpa. I've seen enough old duffers who can't remember that they were once kids.

If you're upset, leave the room. If you have to say something negative, shut your mouth. If you aren't sure if you're grumpy, ask Grandma or your child or a grandkid (preferably one between ages four and six). They'll all be honest. Listen to them.

Teach your grandkids the following song and have them sing it to you. It's to the tune of "Oh My Darling, Clementine,"

I'm a lobster,
I'm a lobster,
I'm a lobster through and through.
But I'd rather be a lobster
Than an old crab like you!

Life

Life is a learning experience, and grandpas have lived more of it than their progeny. The goal is to teach what you've learned to your grandkids. It's too late to teach it to your kids.

> *Life is one grand, sweet song, so start the music.*
>
> Ronald Reagan

For a child, Grandpa should embody life. He should be a pillar of wit and wisdom. You have wit and wisdom, so show it. You have a life. You are interesting. Your grandchildren are part of you. If you don't show them that part of themselves, they may never understand it.

Give them your life story. If you can, write it. If you

can't write, tell it. Tell it a little at a time. Tell it over and over again. Tell it with pictures. Tell it with mementos. Tell it with keepsakes. Tell them *why* you are who you are. Tell them of choices, right and wrong, that made you who you are. Tell them of your parents and grandparents: where they were from, what they did, who they were. Give them a sense of life larger than their own tiny circle. You are the passageway to a world of their family history. I love Robert Frost's "The Road Not Taken." Take your grandchildren by the hand down the road to their future by way of their past.

> *Isn't life beautiful?*
> *Isn't life gay?*
> *Isn't life the perfect thing*
> *To pass the time away?*
>
> The Smothers Brothers

This book reflects my values. If you wrote it, it would reflect yours. I like my values. They're like a well-worn pair of Levis. They fit me. I'm comfortable with them. I wish everyone had them, and I'm not afraid to say so.

I love God, my family, and my country. I was a young adult in the era of hippies, free love, and cries for tolerance. A bumper sticker I've seen reminds me of those days. It says, "A mind is like a parachute: to be effective it must remain open." That's a clever analogy, but it doesn't go far enough. To be effective, a parachute must be open at one end and closed at the other. If it doesn't hang on to some of that air, you'll splat on the ground.

Our minds have been open for a number of years now. Hopefully we've grasped onto some of the good air and let the bad slip away. Hopefully we've kept what has worked for us and for our parents and grandparents. Hopefully we can pass some of that along to our progeny.

I'll expose my values as you read this book. If you don't share them, that's fine. Whatever you hold to be valuable, pass it on. Don't make your grandkids start all over again.

What are the most important values in my life? How can I help my grandchildren understand those values?

Wisdom

I've known that knowledge can be taught but have wondered if wisdom can only be gained. I've concluded that it can be taught to those willing to learn it, but mainly by example. Parents are often too close for children to observe. Parents are often unwise themselves. Fortunately grandpas are all-wise (just ask us). We can play that role by example and by being close by when a child is in need.

When a child needs a listening ear, listen. After you've listened for an hour or so, a child may be open to a single sentence of your wisdom. Never make the mistake of trying

> *With the ancient is wisdom.*
>
> Psalms 12:12

> *I believe that wisdom consists in caring immensely for a few right things and not caring a straw about the rest.*
>
> John Buchan

to impart any more than that. It will be lost.

Teaching wisdom doesn't mean correcting. That is seldom a grandpa's place. When necessary, a quick "don't do that" should suffice. I wasted many a word with my own kids—often letting the conflict become an argument—as I tried to explain why some behavior was unacceptable. If possible, avoid correcting altogether. You don't want to wear that label. If Mom or Dad says no, you might be able to explain later why the action was objectionable to Mom or Dad. A child will tune out the person that said no.

Don't countermand Mom or Dad. It will cause confusion in a child's mind. You can and should hold and hug them when they get in trouble. You shouldn't tell them what they did was all right if their parents saw it as wrong.

Issues of right and wrong can and should be discussed. It is much more effective to do so in a quiet moment, after the storm has passed. An experience from your own life would be helpful in such a situation. If you ever made a similar mistake, let them know. Then tell them how you learned to avoid making it again. If you never made that mistake, tell them of someone who did. If you can invent a whopper with a horrendous outcome, so much the better.

I've been blessed by being exposed to a lifetime of people, places, and things. I've lived in several places, had several careers, and travelled around the world. The greatest lesson I've learned is "It's not what you do, but who you do it with that counts." Unless you're some great leader, you will only touch a small circle of humanity. The innermost circle is your family. Even if you are some great leader, you need to focus on what is most important. No success in worldly pursuits can equal success at home.

What words of wisdom would I like to pass on to my grandkids? How and when can I teach them?

Time

I was born with a strong "time gene." I hate being late. I hate sitting through a meeting that runs overtime. An hour almost always seems like an hour, a day like a day, and I've never felt that the years have flown by. From what everyone else says, I'm unusual in this regard.

While all of the above are true of my own life, they aren't true for others. My grandkids' lives are sailing by all too quickly. I age at less than 2 percent per year. They age up to 100 percent.

> *A child need not be very clever*
> *To learn that "later, dear"*
> *means "never."*
>
> Ogden Nash

As a grandpa,

I've had years go by when I've had to spend lots of time and energy just earning a living. I've had years go by when I could afford neither the time nor the money to visit grandkids that weren't local. At times I didn't have the energy to play, even with those that were local. Baseball games were missed, ice cream cones were not provided, and owies weren't kissed better.

That time is lost. They still love me, but I'll never again have the opportunity to intertwine myself in the years I've missed with them.

Don't wait. You'll be dead all too soon. Spend time with your grandkids even if you don't have it. If you don't have it now, you never will. You're old. Hurry up and take the time to slow down.

How can I make time to be with my grandkids?

Whatever happened to time?
Doesn't come around anymore.
The very last time I saw
Was a-whistlin' out the door.

The Smothers Brothers

Birth

Grandpas are born at the birth of their first grandchild. The birth of a child is an opportunity to center ourselves and our families on eternal things. Don't try to spout wisdom, but be there, be tearful, and be humbled. Let your own child know you are grateful not just for the birth of their child, but also for their own birth. This is a time for the binding together of one generation to another.

> *A child is a curly dimpled lunatic.*
>
> Ralph Waldo Emerson

If this is your first grandchild, take the time to outline the kind of grandpa you'd like to be. (If someone gave you this book, use it.) You'll never accomplish it all, but doing this will help you channel your efforts.

What would you like your grandchild to be? Not in terms of a profession, but as a person. What could you have done better in your own life? Certainly you won't die wishing you could have made more money or achieved more fame. You'll die hoping those you love, love you.

Look at your newborn grandchild and pledge your life to sharing your love with that child. When you're gone, he or she may be all that's left of you.

How can I celebrate the birth of a grandchild? What commitments will I make toward that child?

Babysitting

Babysitting is best left to Grandma, but sometimes you'll be stuck with it. Below are some guidelines for making sure you're not stuck too often:

A characteristic of a normal child is that he doesn't act that way very often.

Unknown

1. Always feed the kids a ton of junk food, especially sugar, unless it's you that is going to have to get them to sleep.
2. Just before the parents return, be sure the kids are still dressed, filled with sugar, and playing chase around the house.

3. Use the TV to entertain them once you're out of breath from reading and giving horsey rides. Right before the parents return, begin a game of tag.
4. When you get stuck with a little one, be sure you leave the poopy diaper on for the parents to change.
5. If you can come up with a gross story of some sort that they'll repeat to their parents, you may disqualify yourself from future duty.

If I were being serious about the good that can come of an opportunity to babysit, I'd go on about songs, stories, and wisdom that could be imparted while at your task. But why be serious about a difficult situation that can be avoided with a bit of grandfatherly guile?

How can I avoid babysitting or ensure I don't get stuck with it again?

My grandkids believe I'm the oldest thing in the world. And after two or three hours with them, I believe it, too.

Gene Perret

Gifts

Toys are the chicken's way out. You can do better than a store-bought toy. My grandkids get inundated with them from parents, Santa, aunts and uncles, other grandparents, and so on. Don't take the easy way out.

The mere volume of toys today is a tragedy. I really do feel sorry for this generation. How many kids remember the toys they got last year? I can remember half a dozen toys from my boyhood. I don't think I had any more than that. Half of those were hand-me-downs. I remember countless hours spent with those few toys. Those hours

> *The only gift is a portion of thyself.*
>
> Ralph Waldo Emerson

were full of imagination and became lifelong memories.

A multitude of toys denigrates the value of any individual item. That said, some toys are better than others. Anything that gets wound up and watched, seldom gets watched after day one. Some toys become obsessions, such as video games. We didn't have that problem when we were kids.

Some toys encourage imagination. Dolls, Legos, blocks, and the like get kids thinking. Balls, fishing poles, or similar items require your ongoing commitment but are worth it. Coloring books and sticker books are one-time use items. They will get used if you join in, and they're cheap. If you give these and don't join in, YOU are cheap. You can find free things that are better than store-bought toys. My kids would spend hours playing in an appliance box when I found one.

It's better to have gifts than receipts.

Tommy Smothers

Books, though not exciting when received, can be enjoyed many times if they're not "grandma books" (see the chapter on stories).

I am somewhat of a woodworker. A few years ago, for Christmas, I made my granddaughters doll cradles and my grandsons wooden swords. Two years ago, my wife gave them individualized fuzzy blankets for TV watching. Last year they got beach towels with their names stitched into them.

For birthdays, give them a meal out at a restaurant, just Grandpa and the birthday child. Give them a kite and a few hours of time to fly it together. Don't give them the latest action figure or talking doll. By next year they'll have forgotten it. Time with you or a customized gift is a forever memory.

What gifts can I give my grandchildren that will create memories?

Food and Mealtime

The fact is, Grandmas are usually the ones who make really good food. Grandpas are in charge of making sure it gets eaten properly. Have you shown your grandkids how many grapes you can fit in your mouth? Have you taught them that it's only proper to eat olives when they're stuck on a finger? Are they aware that sneaking tastes before the meal is served or having dessert first are the norm, not forbidden? Do they know that eating the optimum ratio of ice cream to pie is

> *Vegetables are a must. I suggest carrot cake, zucchini bread, and pumpkin pie.*
>
> Jim Davis

> *As a child my family's menu consisted of two choices: take it or leave it.*
>
> Buddy Hackett

a talent that takes a lifetime of practice? These rules are in the realm of Grandpa's teachings about food.

You should also teach your grandkids about old-time foods. My dad spent some time down South and occasionally fried up some okra for us. We were the only kids in our neighborhood who knew what okra was.

At Christmas a couple of years ago, it dawned on me that though I had always had pomegranates at Christmas, the grandkids probably hadn't. Indeed, at least four of them who were old enough to know about pomegranates, didn't know. I brought some home, and two grandkids liked them.

> *Never work before breakfast; if you have to work before breakfast, eat your breakfast first.*
>
> Josh Billings

What mealtime traditions (aka disgusting food habits) should I help my grandkids develop?

The most remarkable thing about my mother is that for thirty years she served the family nothing but leftovers. The original meal has never been found.

Calvin Trillin

What foods should my grandchildren have the experience of eating?

Red meat is not bad for you. Now blue-green meat, that's bad for you.

Tommy Smothers

Holidays

Family holiday traditions can be treasured for generations. I'll wager you have some. Do your kids and grandkids have them? Although they may have adopted some from the in-laws, you can assure that some of your own get included.

Food can be a tradition. In addition to pomegranates at Christmas, which I mentioned in the mealtime section, we always had grape slushies at Thanksgiving. (These are made by freezing grape juice in ice-cube trays and then putting the cubes in small glasses, pouring lemon-lime soda over them, and crushing the grape-cubes.) Thanksgiving also brought orange tapioca Jell-O and orange frosted dinner rolls. (For recipes, you'll have to wait for the Grandma's Guidebook.)

As a descendant of William Bradford (governor of The Plymouth colony), I subject my family to stories of the Pilgrims before every Thanksgiving meal. Here's how I tell it to the younger ones.

"My great-great-great-great-great-great-great-great-great-great-great-great-great-grandfather was William Bradford.

"That makes him your great-great-great-great-great-great-great-great-great-great-great-great-great-great-great-grandfather.

"He came to America with the Pilgrims on the Mayflower. It was a hard life. He had to leave William Jr. in the Old World, and his wife fell off the boat and drowned just before they landed in the New World.

"The first governor died a couple of months after they arrived, and William was elected to take his place. He was governor of Plymouth colony for more than forty years.

"It was very cold the first year they were there, and they nearly starved. In fact, over half of them died. A friendly Indian named Squanto came along. He spoke English and taught them how to grow corn. The soil wasn't very good, so he told them to plant a dead fish with each corn plant for fertilizer and plant beans that would wrap around the corn stalk as they grew.

"The second year they had a great harvest and felt

ully blessed. William called for a day of Thanks- here were actually more Indians there than Pil-

ause of Great-Grandpa William, all of us take a day each year to show our thanks for the great life we enjoy.

"Now, don't be turkeys, be thankful."

A Christmas tradition at our house was to have the kids dress in bathrobes with towels around their heads and act out the Nativity on Christmas Eve. The grandkids still enjoy acting it out. You may have to gather cousins to assist, but we had six children and could usually make do. The older relatives loved the show.

Traditions can include fireworks on the 4th of July, new clothes on Easter, or a spook house on Halloween. Traditions are anything you have done or can do to make a holiday special to your family. Holidays can be created too. In my family I have become the designated cake baker. Whenever I bake one, we try to come up with a reason for it—the birthday of someone's friend or friend's mother or any other excuse for a celebration.

The world is full of reasons to celebrate—you needn't invent any yourself. Congress and your state legislature have created many holidays for you. Groups and associations often declare their own days, weeks, and months for celebration.

For example, the first Sunday after Labor Day is designated "Grandparents Day" in the United States. The official "Grandparents Day" has an official song, "A Song for Grandma and Grandpa," and an official flower, the forget-me-not.

October 15 is official "White Cane Safety Day" to be celebrated for blind people, those that know blind people, or anyone who holds blind people in esteem.

You may wish to celebrate the birthday of some famous person or find out which famous people were born on your grandchild's birthday. May 26, for example, is neither my birthday nor the birthday of anyone else that I know. But it is the birthday of

- John Wayne
- Jay Silverheels (Tonto in the original Lone Ranger show)
- James Arness (Marshal Matt Dillon in "Gunsmoke")
- Al Jolson (star of the first talking movie "The Jazz Singer")

May also includes "No Socks Day," "Eat What You Want Day," "Dance Like a Chicken Day," and "National Chocolate Chip Day."

March 26 is "National Make Up Your Own Holiday Day."

Some days become classics in and of themselves like

September 19, "Talk Like a Pirate Day." It has its own website, "talklikeapirate.com," which will teach you all about pirates as well as how to talk like one in English, German, and Dutch.

(For an exhausting—but not exhaustive—list of holidays and famous birthdays, see the appendix on holidays.)

What holidays can I celebrate with my grandkids and how will we make our celebrations special?

Work

Teach your grandkids to work, preferably outside. Teach them to interact, to converse, but above all to be active in work. You may be the only one with time to do this.

My own childhood work experience was extensive. Besides yard and housework, I had a paper route from age ten. I also did farmwork outside of town beginning at eight years old and continuing part-way into college. I'm sure many of you have similar stories. It was far

> *Opportunity is missed by most people because it is dressed in overalls and looks like work.*
>
> Thomas Edison

more common fifty years ago.

My children were fortunate. We had an acre of yard. We used home-chopped wood for heat. And we built our own home. Getting them to work was excruciating, but whenever they went to someone else's place or whenever they got a job, people would tell me what great workers they were.

Times have changed. Many young families have no yard at all. Farm labor is not available for most. Minimum wage laws and tougher child labor laws have curtailed many opportunities. These conditions make it imperative that grandpas get involved. Perhaps you have a yard while your children don't. Maybe you have a garden.

> *I'm a great believer in luck. I find the harder I work, the more I have of it.*
>
> Thomas Jefferson

Teach your grandkids perseverance. Talk of years spent at one job or of beginning a business that is now successful. Show them a tree you planted forty years ago. Give them a sense of working, perhaps struggling, over a long period of time. This generation is used to instant gratification, sound bites, movies on demand, and fast food. You should find opportunities to show them long-term results tied to long-term efforts.

Grandpas work, whether they're retired or not.

Gardening, home repair, and community service are all ways of teaching our grandkids to work. If you're not capable of work, have them wait on you. It's their work that's important. You are the vehicle for learning to do it.

How can I teach a work ethic to my grandkids?

Outdoors

Get your grandkids out of the house, away from the TV, the computer, and the Wii. (If you don't know what a Wii is, good for you.) Kids seldom play in their yards anymore. Many have no yards. Only wealthy people can afford them these days. If you have a yard, have the grandkids over and then take them out and play in it. Play whiffle ball or dodgeball or football like you did when you were their age. Kids today only play sports as part of an organized little league. When we were kids, we just got the neighbors together and played in the backyard. Play tag, "no ghosts are out tonight," or kick the can.

If you camp or hike, or if you used to and still can, take the grandkids. Short hikes are okay, maybe to the

Dairy Queen. Camping in the backyard is great. (You can even sneak inside later if you ever get them to sleep.)

Climb a tree or a rock (or at least give them a boost and ooh and aah about how high they are). Walk along a stream. Skip rocks on a lake. Get them to swim in something other than a chlorinated pool. Gaze at the stars with them. Find the Big Dipper. Count shooting stars. Contemplate the universe and God and man.

> *Camping is nature's way of promoting the motel industry.*
>
> Dave Barry

Show your grandkids what mountains, forests, and seas look like. Take them on vacation and stop along the way. Don't just try to get somewhere, try to experience the journey. Drive them from coast to coast or clear across Montana or Texas. Let them experience wide open spaces. I often wonder if those concerned over saving a tree have ever witnessed the millions in our wilderness areas.

Even if you grew up in a city, you were probably a Boy Scout or your parents sent you to camp. These used to be considered character-building experiences. Build your grandkids' characters. Show them what nature has to offer.

What activities can I share with my grandkids in the great outdoors?

School

My dad never finished college. He talked so much about wishing he was a lawyer that both my brothers came to no good and became lawyers.

Not everyone is meant for college, but everyone should be educated. Education can be formal or casual, learned or earned. Highly educated or not, we all went to school, and some of our most profound memories come from our school days.

I tell my grandkids, "When I was in school, teachers could give spankings. We called them 'hacks.'

"In junior high, the male teachers all had their own custom-made paddles. My homeroom teacher had a green one in the shape of a Christmas tree with holes drilled through it. (The holes were there to decrease wind resistance and increase the sting of the hack.)

"If a lady teacher got upset, she would invite you into the hallway and have the neighboring male teacher join you with his paddle. Then you would bend over and grab your ankles and get your hack. It was very painful, especially if you got one during PE class and you hadn't dressed from your shower.

"I never misbehaved in school but sometimes I would get blamed for someone else's deeds. I got seven hacks in seventh grade. I didn't like them, but it was something that could be bragged about. I'm not sure anyone in junior high got more than I did that year, even though I didn't deserve any of them."

Or sometimes I tell my grandkids what made me a hero in fourth grade.

"We used to play a game called four square. I still see it played at schools these days, but we invented it. There are four squares painted on the pavement, and a person stands in each one. When the ball bounces in your square, you have to slap it to another square or you're out and the next person in line gets your square.

"I was really good, maybe the greatest player ever. One day our teacher, Miss Krueger, joined us for a game. She was in the square next to me when, in a flash of sparkling skill, I faked one way and then cut her corner (meaning I bounced the ball quickly through the inside corner of her square).

"Being a young teacher with a competitive nature, she made a futile dive to try to slap at my shot. She fell to the ground, scraping and mangling her knee to a bloody pulp. She screamed, girls cried, big boys fainted, and someone ran for help. Two male teachers had to come and carry her to the nurse's office.

"I became a playground legend."

Seriously, kids should be encouraged to make the best of their education. If they love to read but can't do math, praise their reading skills. If they're not studious, encourage a hobby, like working with their hands, or anything that they can take pride in. Meanwhile, work with them on their reading. Read to them and then have them read to you. College-bound or not, the ability to read can make a big difference in their chances for success.

I had a practice with my children that I've recently begun with my grandkids. I call it "dollar books." I'll choose a book I think is uplifting or educational, usually nonfiction, and say to the kids, "This is a five-dollar book." That means anyone who reads it gets an immediate payment of five dollars from me. Some of my more mercenary children earned a good chunk of change that way.

School should be both fun and educational. I had fun. I wish I had taken better advantage of the educational part.

How can I encourage my grandkids to get a good education?

What great stories can I share about my school days?

Sports

Kids may love sports or hate them. This often has to do with ability. You may also hate them, but they still merit some exposure.

Kids from kindergarten onward play organized sports. I see some problems with "organized" sports. First, they are organized by adults. It takes no childhood initiative. As a kid I was the neighborhood organizer. I would go from house to house, seeing who was available for football, baseball, or tag. Both boys and girls were welcome because we needed all of them to fill the teams. I had to develop my promotional skills to recruit enough players.

The second problem with organized sports is that kids learn very early that they're no good. Personally, it took me a long time to get over imagining hitting the winning home run or catching a touchdown pass because there were no organized sports till at least age ten.

As a kid I was a "tweener." I was the oldest of the young neighbor kids but not quite one of the older neighbor kids. Often when my older brothers and their friends played sports, they needed a "half-a-player" to even out the skill level of the two teams. I got to be that half-a-player. It was a great opportunity to mingle with my brothers and their friends. It also gave me an opportunity to experience the big leagues.

I once attended basketball practice for one of my kids who was in kindergarten, only to hear the coach tell the other kids not to pass the ball to my child. The coach didn't want the ball going to the least-skilled player. That incident got me into coaching.

The third problem with organized sports is that they can really mess with family time. Different aged kids are on different teams. Even in families with two kids, this can lead to a lot of driving around, a lot of missed family dinners, and so on.

There may be no better option to organized sports. Your grandkids shouldn't be left out of society. But to optimize the situation, become involved. Take them to the games and practices yourself. You could relieve your own children, even if they don't deserve it. Attend and cheer loudly. Coach if you're able. Definitely go out for ice cream after the game.

Teach sports history. Show the grandkids a picture of yourself in your tight-fitting-shorts basketball uniform. Tell them about all of your heroics. Let them know that their own skill is inherited. Let them know who Babe Ruth and Wilt Chamberlain were. I once saw an old man interviewed. He had played basketball for James Naismith, the inventor of basketball. When asked what had been the greatest change in the game, he said it was the addition of the "dribble." I still laugh at that. I would never have guessed basketball was once played without dribbling.

What can I share with my grandkids about sports history? How can I enhance their sports experience through my involvement?

Dress and Appearance

Kids these days are often sartorially challenged. Clothes really do make the man, and a kid shouldn't show up for a job interview in baggy pants or in a black overcoat. We need to love them no matter what, but we should be willing to give grandfatherly advice on matters of appearance. They won't listen to their parents. Let us give it a try.

Clothes make the man. Naked people have little or no influence on society.

Mark Twain

As for us granddads, that's a whole different ball game. Our clothes have already made us, or not. My dad was of the generation where "white collar" workers wore suits. He was always in a suit except when doing yard work. When he did physical labor, he wore plaid flannel. When he died, my sister maid quilts for us siblings from squares of Dad's suits and flannels. The suits defined my father.

How will your grandkids picture you: as a man in a suit or a flannel shirt? Or will they see your Bermuda shorts with chicken legs, a unique hat, and a white beard? You have an opportunity to define yourself by your appearance. Are you a cowboy, a sports nut, a farmer, a surfer? Whatever you are, be it. Dress the part. My opinion is that grandpas should be well groomed but with character.

How would I like my grandkids to picture me?

Keepsakes

My wife and I moved recently, and it reinforced a lesson I'd learned earlier: A picture is worthless until it's seen. When we moved, I carried boxes of pictures, journals, notebooks, speeches, career mementos, and many other treasures. My grandkids had seen few, if any, of them. They'll never be seen till I die and my kids ransack my stuff, looking for valuables. That is, unless I do something about it.

I'm not a pack rat. Aside from pictures, there are maybe three boxes of stuff I'd like to keep. What good are they if I never even open those boxes?

I'm not saying litter your home with trinkets. Some grandparents overdo it and are accused of clutter behind their backs. I know because I am guilty of such accusatory gibes.

A good snapshot stops a moment from running away.

Eudora Welty

Websites and screen savers with family photos are great, but websites are typically visited once per occasion. Still pictures are—and I believe ever will be—appreciated because they capture a moment, and a moment carries memories, feelings, and emotions. Display something you are proud of or something that will impart a vision of the past. Don't overdo it. Start with a plaque, a collage of medals, a painting, or anything that is yours that you'd like your grandkids to see.

Pictures should be organized and put in albums that are available on a prominent bookshelf or a coffee table. Your children will most assuredly look through an album featuring them. Grandkids will also look at pictures of their parents or of themselves and their siblings. A family reunion album will be viewed regularly by attendees. Even an album featuring Grandpa and Grandma as youngsters will be of interest.

To ensure they are prized regularly, have them out, again on a prominent shelf or coffee table. If you can't fit them all, rotate them. Take the time to build albums (best if built around a theme, person, or family). Frame or display a memory or keepsake. If you have many, rotate them.

You're old now, so don't wait. Do it today! If you don't display your life, you'll die depreciated.

What pictures and keepsakes can I share with my grandkids?

Manners

It's extremely important how manners are taught. Parents often fail for lack of skill. Grandpas, with their wealth of experience, should be extremely adept at this.

Not interrupting is important, but don't rebuke a child for interrupting you and definitely don't chastise with anger. This concept should only be taught in the third person. For example, "You shouldn't interrupt your mother." You might add, "I never interrupt Grandma. She smacks me if I do."

Treatment of ladies

Grandpa is the best person to teach boys how to open doors and pull out chairs for ladies and to speak kindly to them and not hit them. This can be taught best using a granddaughter as a target. Open her door, pull out her chair, and do it with a bow and a sweep of the hand ala Sir Walter Raleigh. It will be much more memorable and more often mimicked that way.

Table manners

Grandkids need to know that you shouldn't talk with your mouth full. Teach this with an exaggerated aping of what a child just said. Be sure to puff out your cheeks and garble your words.

Saying please and thank you is another critical habit to acquire. I prefer to teach this principle with a song:

There are two little magic words
That will open up doors with ease
The first little word is "Thanks"
And the second little word is "Please"
When you want the butter
Say "Please pass the butter"
Good manners are never out of style
When you get the butter
Say "Thanks for the butter"
Your mommy will be smiling all the while
There are two little magic words
That will open up doors with ease
The first little word is "Thanks"
And the second little word is "Please"

If you repeat this song often enough, the kids will start singing it too until it gets so obnoxious that everyone will form the habit rather than listen to it.

The most important of manners is to treat adults with respect (especially grandpas). This can only be taught by slapping the kid around! Actually, when kids get old enough to understand the word *respect* they'll probably say something like, "He doesn't deserve respect." I've learned to counter that by saying, "Whether he is deserving of respect will determine the type of person he becomes. Whether you treat him with respect will determine the type of person you become."

What manners do I need to teach my grandkids?

Religion

"Nothing is sacred anymore." We've heard that one many times. To an extent, it is certainly true. I've pondered why modern attitudes are what they are. Some people oppose war as if human life was sacred but promote abortion as if life was meaningless. Some seem to value plant or animal life above human life. Some would give their life for a cause; for some, no cause is worth a life.

> *Do not give up the religion of your youth until you get a better one.*
>
> Martin H. Fischer

Certainly if nothing is sacred, there is nothing worth

sacrificing for. The words have the same root. If your country isn't held sacred, you won't fight and die for it. If your family isn't sacred, you will leave when the going gets tough. Your religion becomes whatever is sacred to you. Determine what that is and pass it on.

Religion is a personal subject, so make it one. Most in our generation were raised "religious." If you don't attend church, it's likely your parents or your grandparents did. If you attend church, take your grandchildren. If your kids aren't religious or if your kids are of a different religion, so what? You don't have to ask your grandkids to join your church or believe the same things you do. If nothing else, use your religious practices as a chance for your grandkids to understand their grandpa, a chance to experience culture the way it was, or as a chance for them to compare your religion to their parents' or to none at all.

> *My religiosity consists in humble adoration of the infinitely superior spirit that reveals itself in the little that we, with our weak transitory understanding, can comprehend of reality.*
>
> Albert Einstein

I've heard it said by parents that they don't force religion on their children because they want them to be able to choose for themselves when they are of age. What a cop-out!

Kids are forced by society to face all kinds of modern mores. How will they be able to choose when they're of age if the choices have not been presented to them? The choice in favor of religion will not be offered them on TV or via the Internet. Would you "not force" medical education on your doctor because when he gets you under the knife, you want him to be free to choose his method? Religion, as I believe it, is more a matter of life or death than surgery.

Take your grandkids to church or synagogue or mosque. Read them Bible stories or stories from whatever religion you believe. It is your place to pass on those traditions. It is not your place to force. But it is your place to offer an opportunity for your grandkids to experience what you have enjoyed.

What can I do to share my religion with my grandkids?

Politics

When grandchildren are old enough (typically around two months) you should begin to impart your views on politics. If their parents' views differ from yours, do it quietly or out of range of the parents' hearing. If the entire family is in agreement, feel free to harp away on any news item, politician, or unwanted tax (are there any wanted ones?).

> *Politicians are like diapers. They both need changing often and for the same reason.*
>
> Unknown (but loved)

On the above issue, I say I have the right to complain about taxes, but I still pay them. We have an obligation to our nation to be honest and supportive of its laws. We also have methods in place to make changes when we feel it necessary. I'm sure my political views can be surmised. If you disagree with them, it's too late. Somebody's already paid for this book, and I've been rewarded.

I'm not an activist. I've never run for office. But I have been involved in other people's campaigns, and I always vote. It's okay for grandkids to know you have strong feelings on politics and current events. Involvement in politics is patriotic. Be firm but not dogmatic. Be known as a grandpa with strong opinions, not a stick-in-the-mud.

> *Those too smart to engage in politics are punished by being governed by those who are dumber.*
>
> Plato

What can I pass on about the political process that will give my grandkids a sense of their country's history and ensure their involvement in the future?

We hang the petty thieves and appoint the great ones to public office.

Aesop

Stories: Reading

This is my favorite section.

I'm very picky when it comes to reading stories to my grandkids. I need a story that lets me emote. Traditional stories such as "The Three Bears" or "The Three Little Pigs" are great because you can talk in a wee little baby bear voice or a great big papa bear voice. You can huff and puff with great enthusiasm or you can use your tickle-fingers to gobble your grandkids all up.

> *Outside of a dog a book is man's best friend. Inside of a dog it's too dark to read.*
>
> Groucho Marx

Some of the politically correct fairy tales are tamed up terribly and you may have to ad-lib if you're reading a new edition. If a grandchild brings me a mamby pamby, watered-down, sissy britches, goody-goody book, I'll refuse to read it. "That's a grandma book," I tell them and get one of grandpa's approved stories to read.

Some modern favorites of mine are:

- *Harry and the Terrible Whatzit*
- *Where the Wild Things Are*
- *What Do You Do with a Kangaroo?*
- *Mike Mulligan and His Steam Shovel*
- Almost any book by Dr. Seuss

When you read a children's book, notice how the arrangement of the words on the page give signals for how they should be read. If the words crescendo, that's what your voice should do. If the words bounce up and down or twist around the page, that's what your head, or whole body, should do as you wind up toward delivering your pitch. Belt out exclamations like they're volcanic eruptions. Ham it up. Shock your grandkids. Make their parents ashamed of you. Read stories like no one else will. Be a grandpa.

I'll stop there, but make sure there are growls, grunts, groans, and gotchas in any story you read. Anything less is for grandmas.

Stories approved for grandpa's reading:

Stories: Telling

Telling stories is an art form. I can't claim to be good at it, but campfires and darkness are great props. It's great when the stories you tell have hints of truth to them. If you walked to school as a child, it could have been in five feet of snow and uphill both ways, but you truly did walk to school.

> *I've been through terrible things in my life, some of which actually happened.*
>
> Mark Twain

A favorite one-line story of mine is to take any situation, for instance a grandchild getting a toy, and say "I never had a toy like that when I was a little girl." The kids will respond, "Grandpa, you weren't a little girl."

You may be concerned with promoting gender misidentity issues, but the kids always add something like "girls wear dresses" or "girls have long hair." I think this story tends to reinforce gender identity.

Repetition is important in any grandpa tale. On the way to my parents' house, we used to drive along a stretch of river where as a teenager I sank in a homemade boat. Every time we passed it, my kids heard the story. It had many embellishments but was essentially true. They'll never forget it.

Short comparisons of life then to life now are great to create mental pictures for the grandkids. You can let them know how tough things were as a child when you had to "hike all the way across the room" just to change channels.

When asked to tell a story, I often fall back on a favorite of mine titled: "A Stormy Night in June." I tell this story in a low, slow, eerie voice, and it goes like this:

" 'Twas a stormy night in June, and the ships were out at sea. The captain said, 'Jack, my boy, tell us a story, please.' So Jack began . . .

" 'Twas a stormy night in June, and the ships were out at sea. The captain said, 'Jack, my boy, tell us a story, please.' So Jack began . . .

" 'Twas a stormy night in June, and the ships were

out at sea. The captain said, 'Jack, my boy, tell us a story, please.' So Jack began . . .

This is repeated until the grandkids can take it no more, plus a couple more repetitions for good measure.

Stories of my youth I'd like to pass on:

Action speaks louder than words but not nearly as often.

Mark Twain

Stories: Family History

Grandkids should know their family's history. Their genealogy will give them roots. Where did your progenitors come from? Are you related to anyone famous? Are you related to anyone infamous? Who is the earliest ancestor you knew and what made him or her interesting?

I recently read a biography of Sir Walter Scott, a famous author and poet of the early 1800s. His great-grandfather had a story worth telling.

Sir Walter Scott's great-grandfather was a cattle rustler in Scotland who was once caught in the act by the laird of the estate and sentenced to hang. The lady of the castle objected, saying something like, "You'd hang this handsome lad when I have three ugly unmarried daughters?"

Her husband was persuaded to give the young man an option. If he would marry the oldest girl, he could escape the hangman's noose. According to the story Sir Walter Scott's great-grandfather waited three days until the noose was tied around his neck before he agreed to tie the knot with Meikle Mouth Meg. (Meikle rhymes with tickle and means "much.") In this way Sir Walter laid claim to coming from a noble clan.

In my own family, I have a few interesting tales. My great-grandfather emigrated from England in 1872. He married two sisters (one at a time). The first bore him ten children before she died. The second, the first's younger sibling by nineteen years, was asked to help raise her nieces and nephews and ended up becoming their step-mother. She also bore five children of her own before her poor body wore out.

My great-grandfather's grandfather's brother had the distinction of being the one and only victim of the notorious Onion Pie Murderess. I tell his story like this:

My great-great-great-grandfather had a brother that was killed by the "Onion Pie Murderess" (the title is whispered in a mysterious murderly voice).

His wife fell in love with a younger neighbor. So she decided to do her husband in. In his favorite meal, onion pie, she fed him arsenic by degrees until he died of a supposed sickness. Later the neighbors became suspicious because she spent a lot of time with her new boyfriend. They convinced the sheriff to exhume the body. (That means dig it up).

When they dissected it, the stomach contained traces of arsenic that hadn't been digested yet. This great-great-great-aunt of mine claimed the distinction of being the last woman hanged at the prison in Lewes, Sussex County, England in 1852.

On my mother's side we descend not only from William Bradford (the governor of Plymouth colony), but from Charlemagne, the ancient king of France who descended from the Merovingian kings made famous in the book *The DaVinci Code*. I won't take that one any further.

I hope I'm not boring you with tales of my own ancestry, but I want to encourage you to find out who you descended from. Where did they originate? What did they do? What famous or infamous stories can be told? Studying your family history can become a hobby of yours. Passing it on can become an anchor to your grandkids in an otherwise anchorless world.

Family historical events and people that I can tell my grandkids about:

____

____

____

Love

A grandpa's love should never be conditional. It should not be interrupted by unruly behavior, mess-making, or noisy outbursts. Parents are for discipline. Grandma is for protecting the furniture. School teachers are for the three R's. Grandpas should only teach mayhem, fun, and some serious life lessons that aren't easily gained from less-experienced individuals.

> *The best place to be when you're sad is Grandpa's lap.*
>
> Unknown

I have no trouble saying "I love you" to grandkids or anyone else. If you do, practice in front of a mirror. I do have trouble getting into any long discussions of serious feelings. I can blubber to the extent I'm incomprehensible. I've found that with kids and grandkids, it's much better to express love in writing. It saves me from making a scene and perhaps gives them something to read and remember. Use whatever method is most comfortable for you, but make sure your love is unmistakably expressed.

How can I show love for or cease to push my grandkids away?

> *Children need love, especially when they don't deserve it.*
>
> Harold Hubert

Talents

You have talents, and your grandkids should be aware of them whether your children are or not. These talents don't have to fit under traditional labels like music or art. They are simply the things you do well.

I have a talent for watching movies. It may sound silly, but I want to pass on some of the old classics to my progeny. As my children grew up, the rule was no TV on Sunday except for a movie of Dad's choosing. They were forced to watch *The Sound of Music*, *The Music Man*, *The Court Jester*, and other favorites of mine over and over and over again. Consequently they have a sense of what I grew up on. And when you mention the word *trouble* in our house, it will likely be followed by "right here in River

City." The Sunday movie tradition has been carried on for the grandkids, at their parents' insistence.

I also admit to a talent for reading "really boring books." Kids would never read what I do, but maybe when they inherit my library, they'll wish to see what it was that I saw in those books. I always try to share what I read such as a story from Winston Churchill's life, where an exasperated woman cried, "Winston, if I were your wife, I'd poison your tea!" To which Winston replied, "Nancy, if I were your husband, I'd drink it."[1] This book-reading talent is passed along via the "dollar book" process described earlier in the school section.

Finally I can also admit to a talent for coming up with exactly the right thing to say in a given situation—long after the situation is past.

If you do have a real talent such as music, art, cooking, woodworking, knife sharpening, spitting, or something similar, take some time to share it. Not all grandkids will want to learn it, but genetically the odds are good that there will be one with the same inclinations.

What would you really like to give your grandchildren? I can't tell you how many people—especially women—come into my hardwoods store, sniff the air, and say, "My grandfather was a woodworker. This reminds me of him."

What do you do well? What comes naturally to you? There's a good chance it will come naturally to some of your grandchildren.

Talents I would like to share with my grandkids:

Note

1. William Manchester, *The Last Lion* (New York: Dell Publishing, 1988).

Bedtime

Bedtime is a great time to be a grandpa. The goal is to send the grandkids to bed with giggles and glee. Settling them down to sleep is not your responsibility. Forget about that, and don't be swayed by your children's pleas for sanity.

> *Any kid will run any errand for you if you ask at bedtime.*
>
> Red Skelton

Of course bedtime is story time, but other activities are great as well. A tradition I had with my kids, which I pass on when grandkids sleep over, is called "doop a doop." I put the child on my back and carry him or her to bed saying "doop a doop" and bouncing along with every step I take. When I get in the bedroom, I twirl around, throw the child on the bed, and tickle until he or she can take it no longer.

A second bedtime pastime is to wait until the children are in bed, then clomp slowly and noisily down the hall, growling in a low fairy-tale villain's voice, "Here comes the big bad dad!" (Once I had grandkids, this had to be changed to "Here comes the bad granddad!") This must be played out as long and excruciatingly as possible till you arrive at the bed, where they are cowering under the covers, and tickle them till they can take it no longer.

Some kind of bedtime ritual of riot-causing proportions is a part of any great grandpa's repertoire. Actually getting to sleep is not nearly as critical as creating bedtime memories.

Bedtime traditions I would like to inflict on my grandkids' parents:

Grandma

Grandkids are always interested in historical fiction. Tell them about your courtship. I tell my grandkids:

"When I started dating Grandma, we were in college. Back then girls weren't allowed to come into the boy's dorm except on Sunday afternoons. Even then the doors to the rooms needed to be left open. I invited Grandma to my room when we'd only known each other a couple of weeks.

"As we sat there, one of the guys from down the hall came in and said 'Hi, you must be Nancy.'

" 'No,' Grandma answered, 'I'm Robin.'

"He left, and a few minutes later another guy came in and said, 'Hi, are you Nancy?'

" 'No,' Grandma answered, 'I'm Robin.'

"When a third guy came in and said 'Hi, Nancy,' I got suspicious. I looked out into the hall. My roommate had guys lined up waiting to come in and ask Grandma if she was Nancy.

"I still get a dirty look from Grandma whenever that name is mentioned."

You could also lie and say things like:

"Grandma married me for my looks. I was even more handsome then than I am now. When you grow up, you might be as handsome as I am (or you might marry someone as handsome as I am). Of course, that was before Grandma got her glasses."

"Grandma married me because I was so rich. Then she spent it all."

"Grandma married me because I was the best kisser." When you tell this one, make sure they're looking, take Grandma in your arms, put your hand on her back, tip her parallel to the floor, and give her a big, sloppy, movie kiss. It'll have them in apoplectic giggling fits.

"I married Grandma 'cause she was the prettiest girl in the world, and then she got even prettier."

You should also let them know that Grandma's the boss. (But see rule #1)

Use humor to illustrate your relationship. For example, "Grandma and I split the housework 50/50. She irons, I wrinkle. She cleans, I dirty. She cooks, I eat." (See appendix for more grandpa and grandma jokes.)

How can I show my grandkids my love and respect for their grandma? What memorable courtship experiences can I pass along?

Profanity

Grandpas should never use profanity. Kids get plenty of it from school, TV, and other adults. Grandpas have been around long enough to come up with better vocabularies. They're wiser than that. Grandpas should say things like "I reckon," or "oughta," or "shucks." That kind of language will make you memorable. Of course, your own peculiar vocabulary would be even better.

> *A man's character may be learned from the adjectives he habitually uses in conversation.*
>
> Mark Twain

When I was in high school, a group of us made up our minds not to swear and found that the easiest way was to come up with alternatives. The usuals—shoot, gosh, darn, and so on—were an easy switch but not very fun, so we created our own versions.

One of my friend's big brothers had jokingly labeled the cigarette lighter in his car a "chute release" as if the car were a dragster. Among our group, "shoot" was replaced with "chute release," and we had our own alternative. We also used and abused the word "stank," not as the past tense of stink but as an expletive instead of dang or darn or worse.

For comparison purposes we somehow came up with "snorts." Something could be bigger than, uglier than, or colder than snorts. As I use this with my grandkids, they respond with, "Grandpa, snorts isn't cold at all." To which I'll answer, "See, then it is obviously colder than snorts." The same is true of bigger, uglier, and almost any adjective—with the possible exception of louder than snorts.

There has been an unexpected side benefit to all of this silliness. Using funny expressions instead of profanity works on you till you realize that the anger you're trying to express is kind of silly too. Alternatives to profanity lead to alternatives to anger. When one regularly uses profanity to express anger, the words totally lose their effect. Those that constantly use profanity have nothing to turn to when they are truly angry.

I personally have used mild profanity twice in my adult life. Both times the effect was profound. The hearers knew I never did that. A grandpa should not use profanity and should never get angry. The exception would be the rare case of someone's life or health being in jeopardy.

What words can I use in place of profanity?

Children seldom misquote. In fact, they repeat word for word what you shouldn't have said.

Unknown

Creative Conversation

Create your own vernacular

A family should have a language of its own. Grandpa can be the main source. In our family, "squeet" replaces "let's go eat," and "squate" means "I already ate." A grown-up has become "a dolt" instead of an adult.

Many parents have phrases to see their children off to school or on dates such as: "Remember who you are," (meaning don't do anything to disgrace your family or religion). "Be good," "Be careful," or some other such words are meant to arm the children against the bad world outside the home.

Wanting to be original but not having the intellect to come up with something profound, I've always said

"Don't hit anybody." This phrase has become the standard for grandkids also. Unfortunately on days the car got wrecked or someone got into a fight, the kids always reminded me that I had not said it that day.

One of my daughters, after receiving her first kiss, could think of nothing to say when dropped off but "Don't hit anybody."

Language abuse

Language is full of fun. People are overwhelmed or underwhelmed, but are they ever just "whelmed"? People can be ruthless, but are they ever "ruthful"? People often repeat things, but do they ever just "peat" them? Look in the dictionary under "re" or "dis" or some other prefix, and you'll certainly find some words you can have fun with.

> *If the English language made any sense, lackadaisical would have something to do with a shortage of flowers.*
>
> Doug Larson

Come up with your own crazy words and phrases. They'll make you unique. They'll help you overcome your temper. They'll make you immortal as your words are passed down from generation to generation.

What unique words or phrases can our family share?

If you have nothing to say, say nothing.

Mark Twain

Humor: Traffic Signs and Travel

Whether you're on vacation or going shopping, being on the road is a terrific way for a grandpa to get to know and become endeared to his grandchildren.

I've included a section specifically on traveling and traffic signs because most grandpas get opportunities to be in a car with the grandkids.

There are the traditional games, of course, such as finding the alphabet in order on signs or "slug-bug," where you get to slug a fellow passenger for every Volkswagen Beetle you see. Our family has expanded that one to slugging for an out-of-state license plate, but the state must be named before slugging. We also play "Popeye" when driving at night, when license plates and slug bugs aren't as obvious. A "Popeye" is a vehicle with only one headlight.

Besides games, there are endless varieties of humor housed in traffic signs. These are a vast untapped reservoir of grandfatherly wit. Jokes like the ones below can bring smiles and also teach kids to be aware of signs, a habit for which their parents will be grateful when the grandkids reach sixteen.

> *In America there are two classes of travel—first class, and with children.*
>
> Robert Bentley

- "Stop Ahead." Reach over and hold back someone's forehead.
- "Roundabout Ahead." Zip your finger round and round someone's head.
- "Construction Ahead" means to begin digging with your fingers into the head of the person next to you.
- "Left Turn Ahead," "Right Turn Ahead," or anything "Ahead," is a likely opportunity for some chicanery.
- "Shoulder Closed" or "No Shoulder." Scrunch your shoulders together.
- An "S" curve sign means to begin wiggling in your seat.

- An "S curve 20 mph" sign means wiggle at twenty miles per hour.
- "Curve Right" or "Curve Left." Lean right or left.
- "Watch for Ice." Read this sign only in the summer.
- "Crosswalk." Ask, "Why is the walk angry?"
- "Stop Here on Red" is often indicated, but the line is never red, it's white.
- "Dead End" is way too easy. "People are dying to live there" or "There's a cemetery down that road" or many other easy–to–ad-lib comments can be made.
- "No Outlet" is "Dead End" euphemized. "They can't use electricity on this street. The power lines go in, but there's no outlet."
- "Watch for Rolling Rocks" As a Boy Scout I was told the story of how two Indians, "Little Bear" and "Rolling Rocks" went hunting. Rolling Rocks never returned, prompting his friend to post signs along all of the mountain trails.
- "Railroad Crossing" invites the old riddle "Railroad crossing, look out for the cars, can you spell that without any R's?" "Of course you can: T-H-A-T."

Some unusual signs invite unusual humor. When my children were young, going to Grandpa's house entailed traversing a bridge with a sign designating the

Stillaguamish River. Every time we crossed, I'd say "See that river? It used to be a Guamish and it's Still-a-Guamish." Of course before long, the kids would say it before I could, and it became a family tradition.

I regularly pass a sign for "Saybrook Lane" on my way to town, upon which I say, "Brook Lane." Wapato is the name of a town we passed on the road to my parents' home. The town is pronounced "Whop-a-toe" so each time we passed, I would whop someone's toe.

Are there any traffic signs I can make fun of that the author hasn't already copyrighted?

Humor: Jokes

Jokes are part of any grandpa's repertoire. Still, care must be taken. Never tell a joke that denigrates anyone but yourself—not Grandma, not the grandkids, not another race, or anything like that.

Kids are very impressionable and sensitive. I used to use vegetable epithets like "pickle nose" or "lettuce lips" until I found that a three-year-old grandson had taken one of my jokes personally. I had to stop. Quips or one-liners about grandkids should be only positive. It's great to call yourself a "pickle nose" or to joke about your own looks, but not the children's.

> *Wit is educated insolence.*
>
> Aristotle

Comparisons among children should not be made. With two grandsons, if you tell one he's fast and the other he's strong, the first will think he's not strong and the second he's not fast. Compliments should be given as follows: "You're smart because your grandpa is so smart." Or "You're pretty because your grandpa is so handsome." Any positive trait can be attributed to grandpa's side of the family.

The jokes grandpas tell should be the kind that elicit "Oh, Grandpa. That's lame" and similar comments. These kinds of jokes are too simple and too dumb to be noted here. I have, however, included a number of jokes about Grandpa and Grandma in the appendix that can be shared.

Jokes I'd like to tell my grandkids:

Poetry

Grandpas should have a favorite poem or two to share with their grandchildren. They can be comic or serious. My father had a short one:

"A skunk sat on a stump
And the stump thunk the skunk stunk."

Non-rhyming, off-the-wall endings are memorable:

"If a task is once begun,
Never leave it till it's done.
Be the labor great or small,
Do it well or don't do it."

Tommy Smothers

Life is so fast-paced that poetry is lost on this generation. It had only a finger-hold in ours. Take the time to slow down. Take some story time and share some poetry.

I've listed a few of my favorite poems here:

The Raven by Edgar Alan Poe

Though somewhat haunting, I like to read "The Raven" by Edgar Allen Poe. It's riveting and gives you a chance to use and explain words like *quoth* and *pallid*.

I also like this poem because it can be read with deathly whispers and it lets me act all spooky. Besides, I think the sounds and words are the most ghastly, ghoulish, and titillating ever written.

Once, in a college English class, my daughter related how I'd read this to her, and her classmates said I must be quite macabre.

Paul Revere's Ride by Henry Wadsworth Longfellow

On the serious side, I like "Paul Revere's Ride," perhaps because it begins, "Listen, my children, and you shall hear," but also because it instills an interest in history. Grandpas should love history. Grandpas are history.

This poem lets me emote in both whispers and gallops, but it also promotes a sense of the excitement of history.

Jabberwocky by Lewis Carroll

I like to tell my grandkids that any story or movie is

scarrrry (spoken in a frightened whisper). In this case they ask what a Jabberwocky is, and I tell them (in a frightened whisper) "I don't know. That's what makes it so scary."

If by Rudyard Kipling

I love this poem for the lessons it teaches. You may have to explain verse-by-verse what that lesson is—assuming you can figure it out.

In preparing for this book, I looked on the Internet for grandpa-related poems. There were many lines of verse but few that would qualify as poetry. (I also found it striking that most were written as a memorial to a dead grandpa.)

What poetry or verses should I share with my grandkids?

A poem begins with a lump in the throat.

Robert Frost

Songs

There is no excuse short of dumbness for a grandpa not to sing.

If you're a good singer, share it with the grandkids. If you can't carry a tune in a bucket, it's okay. In fact, singing off-key is a prerequisite to many grandpa songs.

> *Never try to teach a pig to sing. It wastes your time and it annoys the pig.*
>
> Anonymous

Riding in the car is a great time for singing because the kids can't run away. Simple, funny songs are the best. I've included a few of my favorites in this book. (See appendix: Songs)

Songs can be used to reveal your feelings. "I Love You a Bushel and a Peck" can be sung over and over without grandkids tiring of it. "You Are My Sunshine" will also show your love and be passed on from one generation to the next. My kids learned a song in church that names each child, mentions the parents, and concludes, "We are a happy family." Find a song that implies love and share it with your grandkids.

Songs I'd like to sing with my grandkids:

Music

As opposed to songs, music is a much broader field. If you refuse to sing or don't know any songs worth sharing, try to share musical eras or genres.

Growing up, my Saturday nights were spent with Lawrence Welk or in my bedroom. It was extremely corny, even in the fifties and sixties, but most of the music was from my parents' generation. It gave me a foundation for knowing the difference between what they listened to and rock and roll. Incidentally, what we called rock and roll is now called oldies.

> *When words leave off, music begins.*
>
> Heinrich Heine

When my kids were adolescents, they preferred to listen to their music as we drove in the car. I preferred talk radio. We compromised on oldies. They love oldies to this day and claim that no one in their generation knows oldies music as well as they do.

If possible, pass on music from your parent's generation. My youngest daughter was once the only one in a music class to know who Al Jolson was. Once I introduced her to Louis Armstrong, she became a fan. At one point she had ten Louis Armstrong CDs, more than she had of any other group or artist.

> *An Intellectual is someone who can listen to the William Tell Overture without thinking of the Lone Ranger.*
>
> John Chesson

Being a nut for musicals myself, my kids learned by heart all of the songs from *The Music Man*, *The Sound of Music*, *Oklahoma*, *South Pacific*, and a number of other shows. My grandkids are on their way to doing the same.

When you drive, while you're around the house, or as you watch the boob tube, make sure that music from the past is featured. Your grandkids deserve the knowledge of how Grandpa boogied when he was a kid.

Music I'd like my grandkids to hear:

The End

In the end, grandfathering, like any other pursuit, has costs and benefits. The costs are time, a sense of humor, a sense of life, and a bit of forethought that this book hopes to help you harvest. The benefits can be grandchildren that give you unbridled love and that are left with a net full of the beauties of life you have helped them gather.

> *It doesn't matter who my father [or grandfather] was, it matters who I remember he was.*
>
> Anne Sexton

I have meant this book to be self-help. I've shared my own experiences not to brag but to inspire. You have surely had just as many wonderful experiences of your own. I'll reiterate that this book represents not the grandpa I am, but the grandpa I'd like to be.

Be the grandpa you'd like to be. Choose a few of the actions this book has inspired in you and make them habits. Be a great grandpa!

Appendix: Holidays

• • • • • • • •

Listed below are websites (ask a grandchild if you don't know what a website is or how to access one) that list many other holidays and birthdays:

Weird Holidays
holidayinsights.com
angelfire.com/falcon/flamingchickens/weird_holidays
thinkquest.org

Famous Birthdays
Famousbirthdays.com
Historyorb.com
Celebritycafe.com/birthdays
Celebritorium.com
Famouslikeme.com

Funforbirthdays.com/birthday

Eforu.com/birthdays (for historical persons, kings, queens, and so forth)

International Holidays

Wikipedia.org/wiki/list_of_holidays_by_country

Brownielocks.com

Most countries have websites that list their holidays.

United States federal observances are days, weeks, months, or other periods designated by the United States Congress for the commemoration or other observance of various events, activities, or topics. These observances differ from Federal holidays in that Federal employees only receive a day free from work on holidays, not observances. Federal observances that are designated by Congress appear in Title 36 of the United States Code (36 U.S.C. § 101 et seq.). Below is a list of all observances so designated. Note that not all of the laws below require that the observance be declared; in some cases, such as 36 U.S.C. § 114, Congress simply requested the President to issue a proclamation of the observance.

The President may also declare selected Federal observances by presidential proclamation. Those observances are referenced as the list of observances in the United States by presidential proclamation.

DAYS

Holiday	Date
Carl Garner Federal Lands Cleanup Day	First Saturday after Labor Day
Child Health Day	First Monday in October
Constitution Day and Citizenship Day	September 17
Columbus Day	Second Monday in October
Father's Day	Third Sunday in June
Flag Day	June 14
Gold Star Mother's Day	Last Sunday in September
Law Day, U.S.A.	May 1
Leif Erikson Day	October 9
Loyalty Day	May 1
Memorial Day	Last Monday in May
Mother's Day	Second Sunday in May
National Aviation Day	August 19
National Day of Prayer	First Thursday in May
National Defense Transportation Day	Third Friday in May
National Freedom Day	February 1
National Grandparents Day	First Sunday in September after Labor Day
National Korean War Veterans Armistice Day	(Was July 27 of each year until 2003)
National Maritime Day	May 22
National Pearl Harbor Remembrance Day	December 7

Holiday	Date
Pan American Aviation Day	December 17
Parents Day	Fourth Sunday in July
Peace Officers Memorial Day (in honor of federal, state, and local officers killed or disabled in the line of duty)	May 15
Stephen Foster Memorial Day	January 13
Thomas Jefferson's birthday	April 13
White Cane Safety Day	October 15
Wright Brothers Day	December 17
Patriot Day	September 11

WEEKS

- Constitution Week
- Days of Remembrance of the Victims of the Holocaust
- National Flag Week
- National Forest Products Week
- National Friendship Week
- National Poison Prevention Week
- National Safe Boating Week
- National School Lunch Week
- National Transportation Week
- Police Week
- Save Your Vision Week

Months

Holiday	Dates
Asian Pacific American Heritage Month	May
Black History Month	February
Breast Cancer Awareness Month	October
Cancer Control Month	April
Confederate History Month	April
Child Abuse Prevention Month	April
National Disability Employment Awareness Month	October
Gay and Lesbian Pride Month	June
American Heart Month	February
National Hispanic Heritage Month	September 15 through October 15
Honor America Days	The twenty-one days from Flag Day through Independence Day
National Nutrition Month	March
Steelmark Month (honors the steel industry)	May

Appendix: Songs

The Grandfather Clock

"The Grandfather Clock" is based on a true story. Over one hundred years ago in Piercebridge, North Yorkshire, England, there was a lodge known as the George Hotel. It was managed by two brothers. In the lobby stood a clock that kept very good time.

One day one of the brothers died, and suddenly the old clock started losing time. At first it lost fifteen minutes a day, but after several clock repairmen gave up trying to fix it, the clock was losing more than an hour each day.

At the death of the second brother, even when fully wound, the clock stood completely stopped.

The new manager of the hotel never attempted to have it repaired. He just left it standing in a sunlit corner of the lobby, its hands resting in the exact position they assumed the moment the second brother died.

Around 1875 an American songwriter named Henry Work happened to be staying at the hotel. He was told the story of the old clock and, after seeing the clock for himself, decided to compose a song about the fascinating coincidence that the clock stopped forever the moment its elderly owner passed away. Henry came back to America and published the lyrics that sold over a million copies of sheet music about the clock.

Since the publishing of the song, what once were known as "floor clocks" have been known as "grandfather clocks."

I'M MY OWN GRANDPA

This song was inspired by an anecdote that has been published periodically by newspapers for well over 150 years and was referred to by Mark Twain. The earliest known mention of the story was recorded in the *London Literary Gazette* in the early 1800s. The song involves a singer, his father, a mother, and her daughter.

The singer marries the older woman.

The older woman's daughter thus becomes his stepdaughter.

Subsequently, the singer's father marries the younger woman.

The younger woman, being the new wife of the singer's father, is now both the singer's stepdaughter and his stepmother. Likewise, the singer's father, being his stepdaughter's husband, is now also his stepson-in-law.

The singer's wife, being the mother of his stepmother, is now both his spouse and his stepgrandmother.

The husband of the singer's wife would then be the singer's stepgrandfather. Since the singer is that person, he has managed to become his own stepgrandfather.

The song continues with the singer and his wife having a son.

The singer's son immediately becomes the stepbrother of the singer's stepdaughter.

Since his stepdaughter is also his stepmother, the singer's son is also his own stepuncle because he is the stepbrother of his stepmother.

The singer's son is now also a brother-in-law to the singer's father because he is the stepbrother of the singer's father's wife.

The singer's father and his wife (the singer's stepdaughter) then have a son of their own.

The child becomes the singer's grandson because he is the son of his stepdaughter.

The son also becomes the stepbrother of the singer because he is the stepson of his own father.

The song "I'm My Own Grandpa" was written by Dwight Latham and Moe Jaffe and was originally performed by Lonzo and Oscar in 1947. Other versions have since been performed by many artists.

THE BEAR WENT OVER THE MOUNTAIN:

(To the tune of "For He's a Jolly Good Fellow")
Oh, the bear went over the mountain
the bear went over the mountain
the bear went over the mountain
To see what he could see.
And all that he could see,
And all that he could see,
Was the other side of the mountain,
The other side of the mountain,
The other side of the mountain,
Was all that he could see.

Bill Grogan's Goat

Bill Grogan's Goat (repeat),
Was feelin' fine (repeat),
Ate three red shirts (repeat),
Right off the line (repeat).
Bill took a stick (repeat),
Gave him a whack (repeat),
And tied that goat (repeat),
To the railroad track (repeat).
The whistle blew! (repeat),
The train . . . grew . . . nigh (dramatic stretch)(repeat),
Bill Grogan's Goat (repeat),
Was doomed to die (repeat).
He heaved a sigh (repeat),
Of . . . aw-ful . . . pain (dramatic stretch) (repeat),
Coughed up the shirts (repeat),
And flagged the train! (repeat).

There's a Hole in the Bottom of the Sea

There's a hole in the bottom of the sea (x2)

Chorus:
There's a hole, there's a hole
There's a hole in the bottom of the sea

There's a log in the hole in the bottom of the sea (x2)

Chorus

There's a branch on the log in the hole in the bottom of the sea (x2)

Chorus

There's a bump on the branch on the log in the hole in the bottom of the sea (x2)

Chorus

There's a frog on the bump on the branch on the log in the hole in the bottom of the sea (x2)

Chorus

There's a wart on the frog on the bump on the branch on the log in the hole in the bottom of the sea (x2)

Chorus

There's a speck on the wart on the frog on the bump on the branch on the log in the hole in the bottom of the sea (x2)

Chorus

There's a fleck on the speck on the wart on the frog on the bump on the branch on the log in the hole in the bottom of the sea (x2)

Chorus

There's a chigger on the fleck on the speck on the wart on the frog on the bump on the branch on the log in the hole in the bottom of the sea (x2)

Chorus

There's some pants on the chigger on the fleck on the speck on the wart on the frog on the bump on the branch on the log in the hole in the bottom of the sea (x2)

Chorus

There's a pocket on the pants on the chigger on the fleck on the speck on the wart on the frog on the bump on the branch on the log in the hole in the bottom of the sea (x2)

Chorus

There's a needle in the pocket on the pants on the chigger on the fleck on the speck on the wart on the frog on the bump on the branch on the log in the hole in the bottom of the sea (x2)

Chorus

There's a thread in the needle in the pocket on the pants on the chigger on the fleck on the speck on the wart on the frog on the bump on the branch on the log in the hole in the bottom of the sea (x2)

Chorus

There's a knot in the thread in the needle in the pocket on the pants on the chigger on the fleck on the speck on the wart on the frog on the bump on the branch on the log in the hole in the bottom of the sea (x2)

Chorus

(This song can go as long as you'd like!)

Appendix: Jokes

Kid: Grandpa, How much does it cost to get married?
Grandpa: I don't know. I'm still paying for it.

> *All men make mistakes, but married men find out about them sooner.*
>
> Red Skelton

Kid: Grandpa, what was the name of the lady that used to live next door?
Grandpa: Let's see. Help me out: I need the name of a flower.
Kid: Tulip, Daisy . . .
Grandpa: No, no, it's the one with the thorny stem.
Kid: Rose?
Grandpa: Yeah, that's it. [Turning to Grandma] Rose, what was the name of that woman that used to live next door?

Grandma: Grandpa's always helped with the houseclean-ing. He lifts his legs so I can vacuum under them.

Kid: Grandma, Grandpa's gasping for breath and calling your name!
Grandma: I guess I didn't hold the pillow down long enough.

Kid: What do you call a man that's lost 95 percent of his brain power?
Grandma: A widower.

If a Grandpa says something in the forest and Grandma's not there to hear it, is he still wrong?

A kid is showing a friend around the family's brain store.
"Wow, this one's $100,000."
"Yeah, it's George Washington's brain."
"This one's $500,000."
"Yeah, it's Einstein's brain."
"This one's $1,000,000."
"Yeah, that's Grandpa's brain. Grandma says it was never used."

Kid: Grandma, why does Grandpa always act like an idiot?
Grandma: He's not acting.

After Grandpa had his physical, Grandma went in to talk to the doctor.
"Ma'am," said the doctor, "he's in bad shape. The only way to prolong his life will be to make him a nutritious meal for breakfast, lunch, and dinner; to always treat him kindly; and to never lose your temper."
As they were driving home, Grandpa asked what the doctor had said.
Grandma answered, "He said you're going to die."

Grandma: When we were first married, you took the small steak and left me the large one. Why don't you do that now? Don't you love me anymore?
Grandpa: Of course. You're just a better cook now.

Kid: Grandpa, it looks like Grandma's mind is completely gone.
Grandpa: Of course it is. She's been giving me a piece of it every day for fifty years.

Kid: Grandpa, I read that the average husband only speaks to his wife thirty-seven minutes per week.
Grandpa: It doesn't take long to say, "Uh-huh," "Yes, dear," and "I'm sorry."

Grandpa: Doctor, my wife sent me in 'cause I can't work around the house.
Doctor: I've checked you out thoroughly. There's nothing

wrong with you. You're just lazy.
Grandpa: Okay, but what's the medical term for that so I can tell my wife?

Grandpa: You're driving me crazy.
Kid: Grandpa, you could walk that far.

Boss: After you left to go to your grandpa's funeral, he stopped by to see you.

Kid: Grandpa, I just got my license. Want to go for a ride?
Grandpa: Sure, if I can sit in back.
Kid: Why would you want to sit in back?
Grandpa: I want to kick the back of your seat like you always did to mine.

Kid at family reunion: Grandpa, what's the name of your brother's daughter?
Grandpa: Denise.
Kid: How about his son?
Grandpa: Denephew.

Kid: Grandpa, let's go to a movie.
Grandpa: How much does it cost?
Kid: Eight dollars.
Grandpa: When I was a kid, the movie was five cents and the popcorn a penny.
Kid: Then you'll really enjoy this one! They have sound now.

Grandpa to teenager: The greatest thing about living this long is you have no more peer pressure.

Teenager golfing with Grandpa: How should I play around this tree?
Grandpa: When I was your age, I just hit right over it.
(Kid tries but fails.)
Grandpa: Of course when I was your age, the tree was only three feet tall.

First kid: Is your grandpa still alive?
Second kid: We think so. At age sixty he started walking five miles a day. We just don't know which direction he went.

You know you're old when you go to an antique auction and three people bid on you.

Kid: My grandpa needs instant replay because he forgets what happened.

Grandpa's teeth are like the stars—they come out at night.

Kid at show and tell: When I went to visit my grandpa's grave, I looked in, and he was seated at a piano using an eraser on some sheet music.
Teacher: That's hard to believe. What did he say he was doing?
Kid: Decomposing.

Kid: Grandpa, I'm in the school play. I play the part of a man that's been happily married for thirty years.
Grandpa: Keep at it, son. Maybe next time you'll get a speaking part.

About the Author

Lorin Barber has an MBA from the University of Washington and a bachelor's degree in Japanese language. He has had a successful career as a manufacturing executive. He has six children and, so far, eight grandchildren. He lives in a small town in the state of Washington with his wife of thirty-six years. In his spare time you might find him panning for gold in the wilds of Washington. This is his first publication.

Lorin would love to hear from his readers via facebook or through email: lorin@lorinbarber.com.

0 26575 53573 0